Trace each color word. Color the pictures.

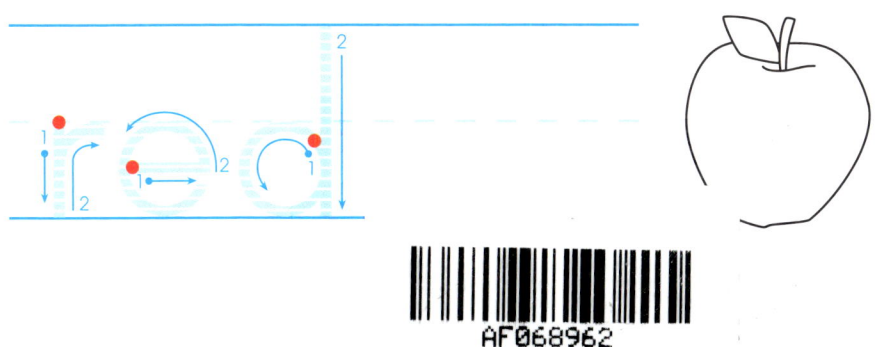

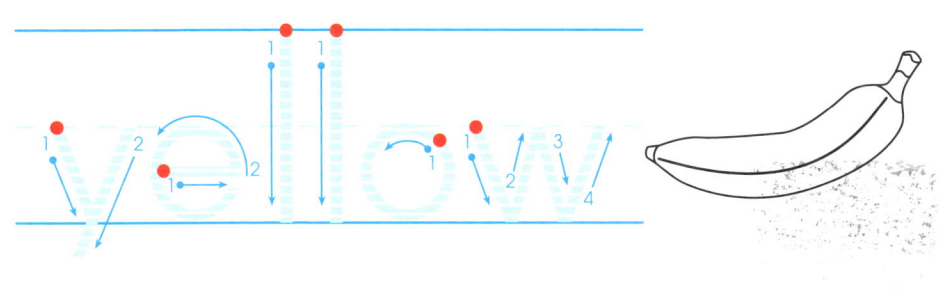

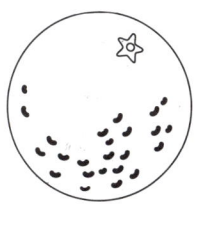

Trace each color word. Color the pictures.

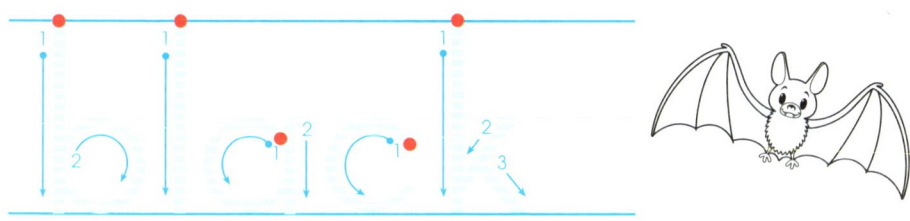

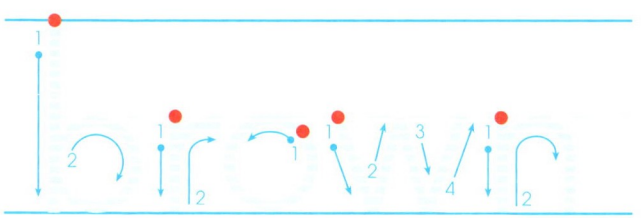

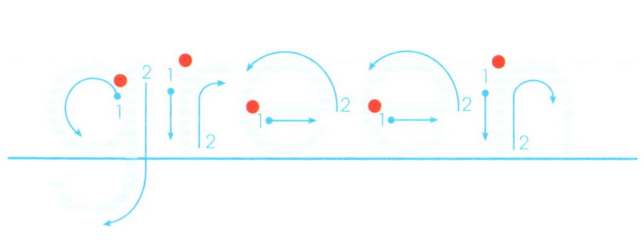

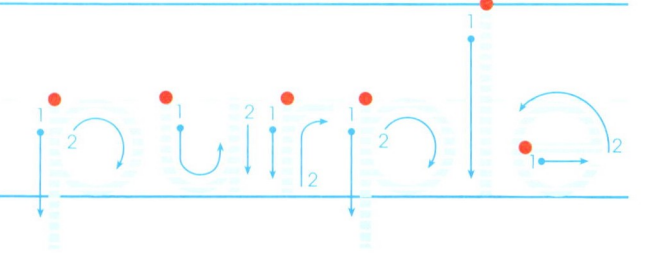

Draw lines between the fish that are the **same**.

In each row, circle the picture that is **different**.

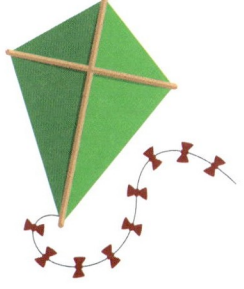  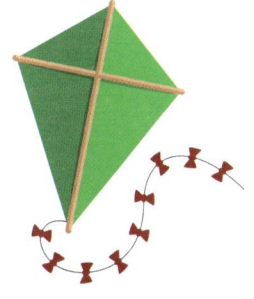

Count the shapes. Write the numbers.

 triangles

 squares

 circles

Draw lines between the butterflies that are the **same size**.

Circle 3 things that **belong** at the beach.

In each row, cross out the picture that **does not belong**.

Draw lines to match the words that **rhyme**.

one

sun

frog

bat

rain

dog

cat

train

Draw lines to match the words that **rhyme**.

star

key

bee

car

fox

fan

can

box

Draw lines to match the **opposites**.

full

off

up

empty

on

out

in

down

Draw lines to match the **opposites**.

day

little

dry

hot

cold

wet

night

big

Help restock the roadside stands.
Draw lines to show where the items **belong**.

Help clean up the garage.
Draw lines to show where the things **belong**.

Draw lines to match the mittens.
Which mitten **does not** have a match? Circle it.

Draw lines to match the socks.
Which sock **does not** have a match? Circle it.

Draw lines to match the shapes.

Draw lines to match the shapes.

Circle what comes next in each pattern.

Draw what comes next in each pattern.
Color your patterns.

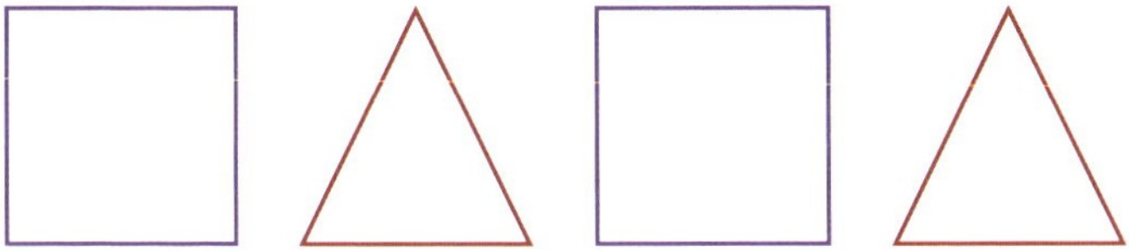

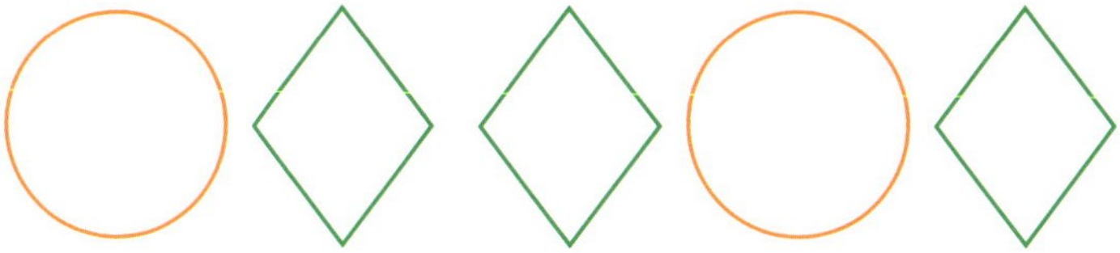

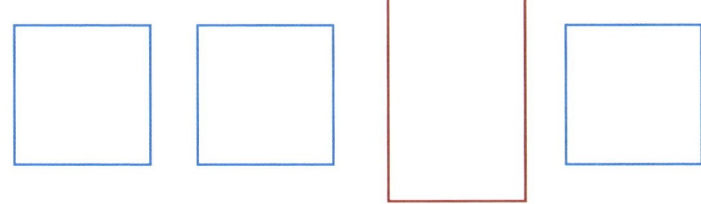

Find and circle the pictures.

shells pail crab sun boat bird

Find and circle the pictures.

pig   chicks   hay   corn stalks   cat   apples

Trace the numbers.

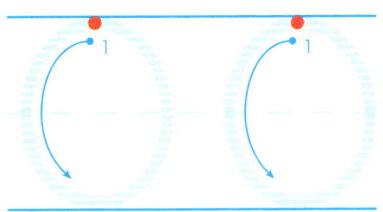 **zero**

This plate has **0** hot dogs on it.

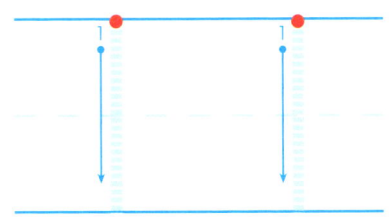 **one**

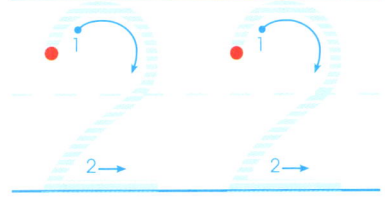 **two**

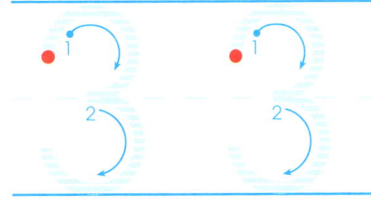 **three**

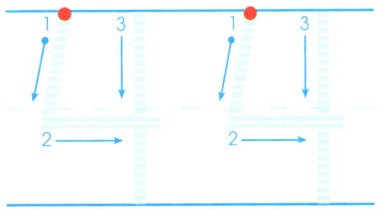 **four**

Trace the numbers.

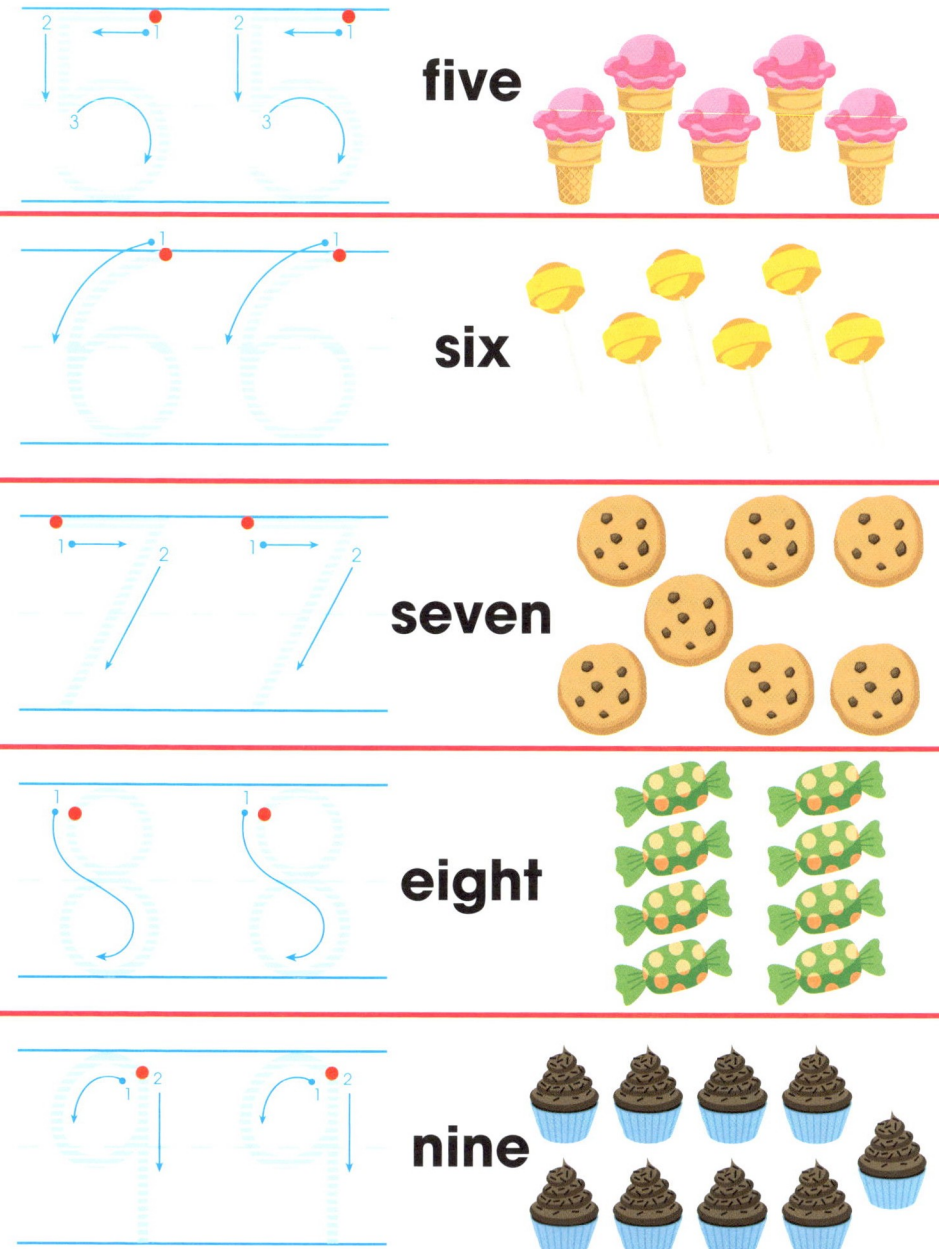

| 2 (4) 3 1 | 5 (6) 4 7 |

How many are there? Circle the numbers.

3   1   5   2

2   5   7   4

1   6   2   4

5   7   3   6

6   4   5   7

5   4   8   7

How many are there? Circle the numbers.

How many are there? Circle the numbers.

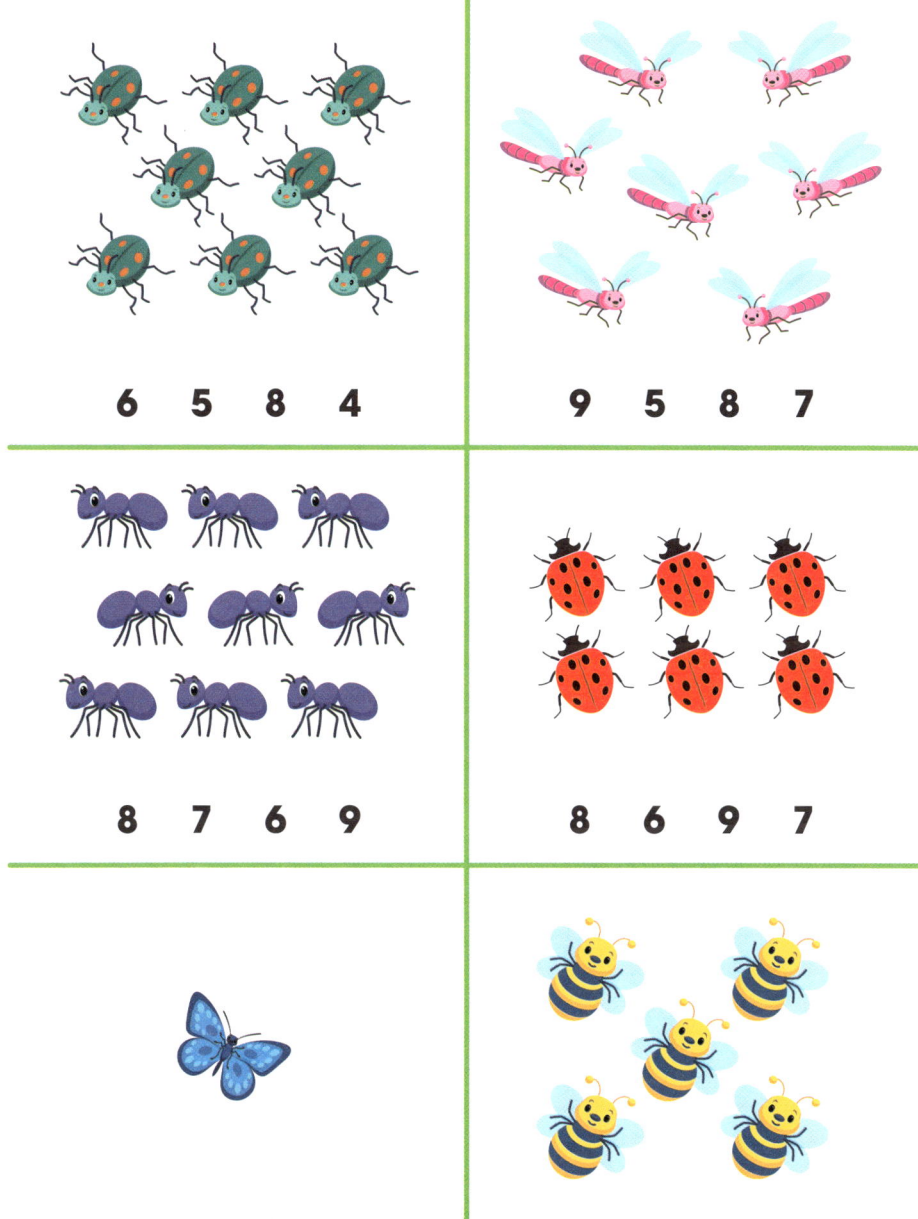

Count the objects in each set. Write each number.
Color each set.

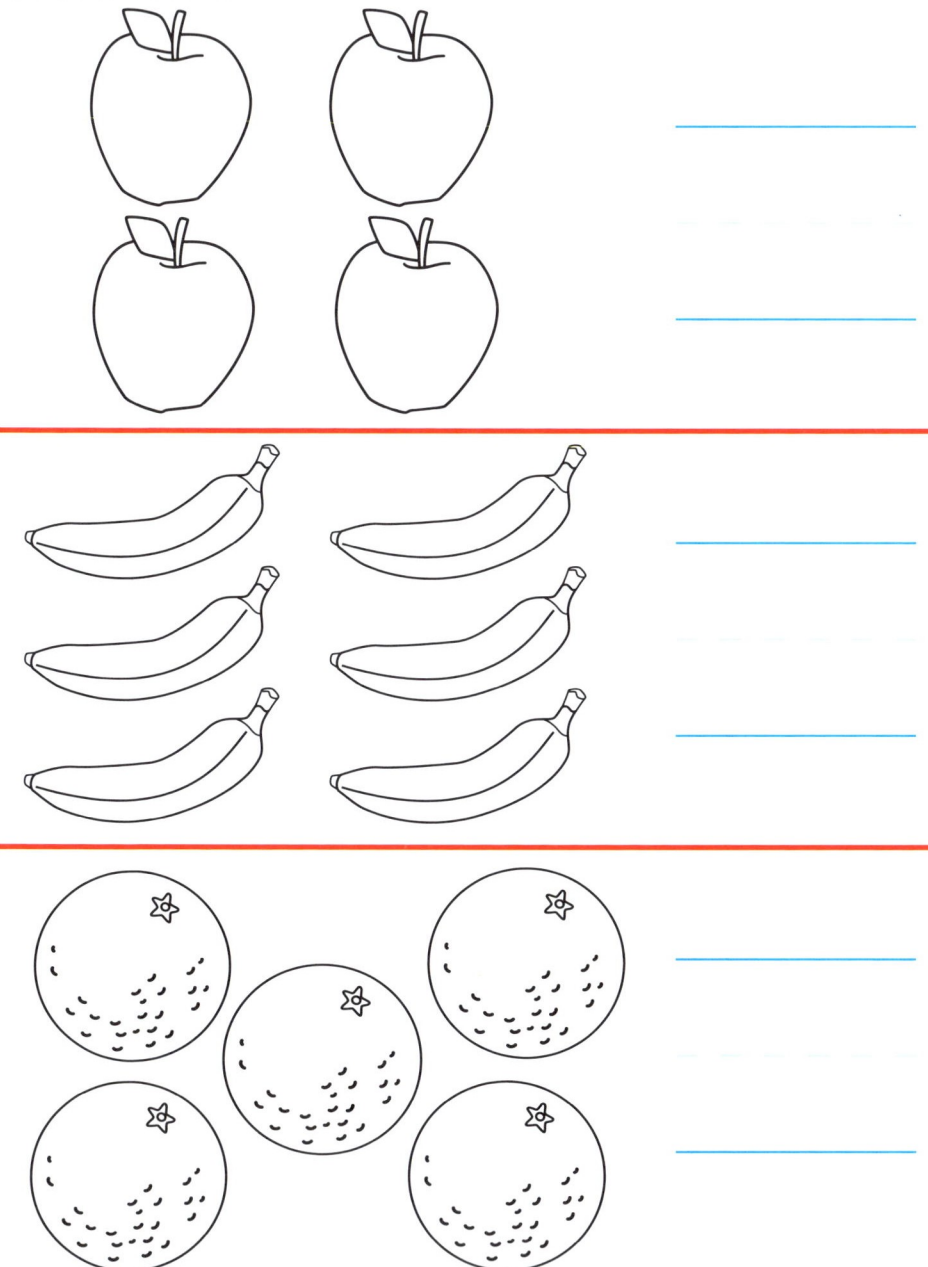

Count the objects in each set. Write each number.
Color each set.

Write how many there are.
Circle the set that has **more**.

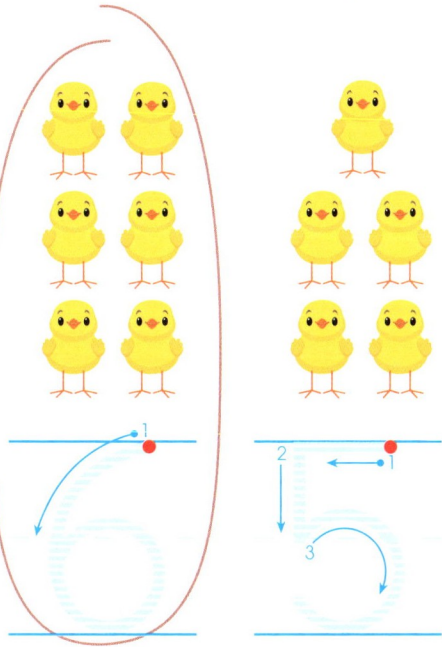

Write how many there are.
Circle the set that has **less**.

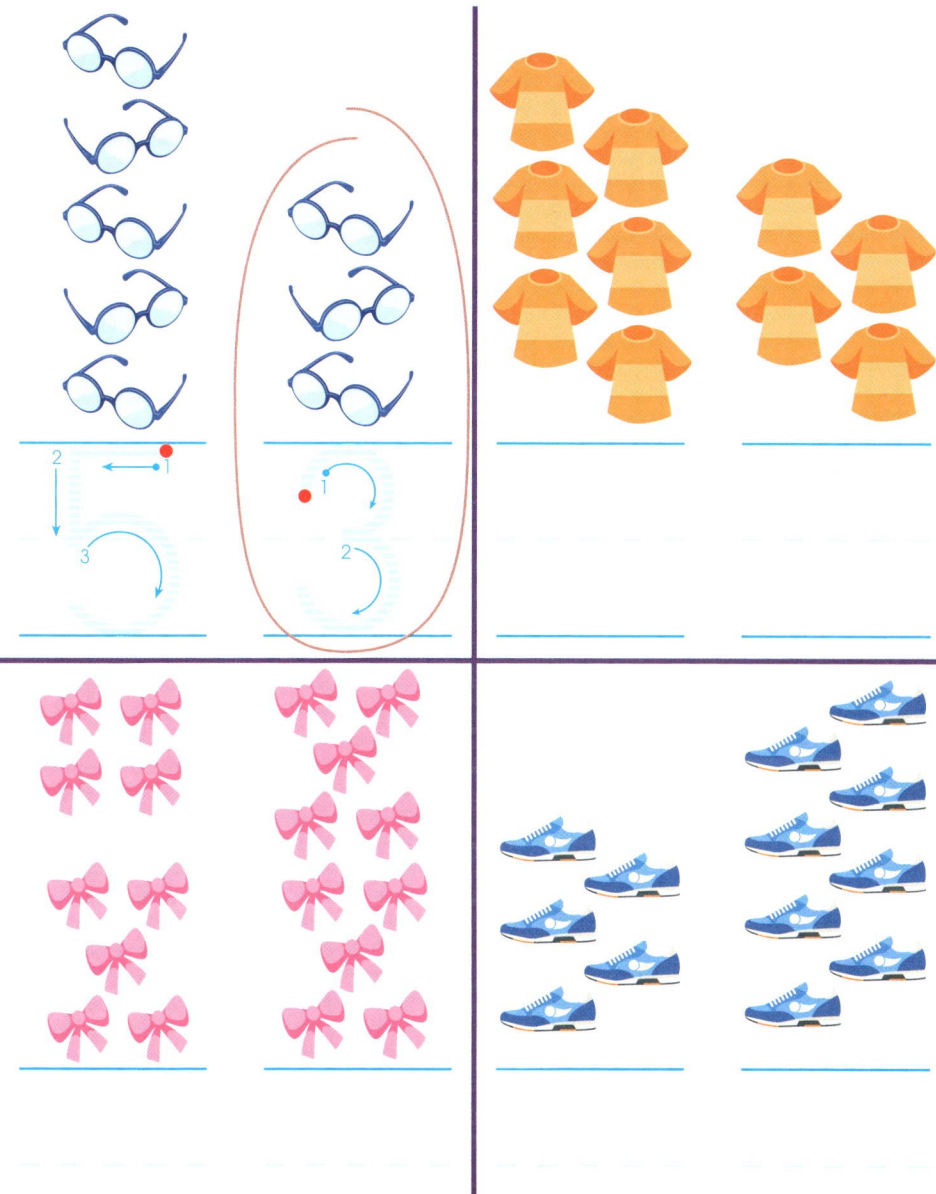

A clock has two hands.
The short hand is the **hour hand**.
The long hand is the **minute hand**.

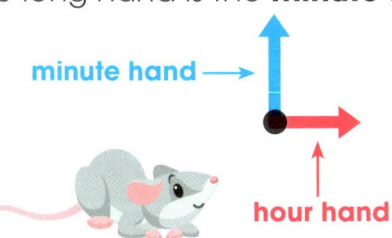

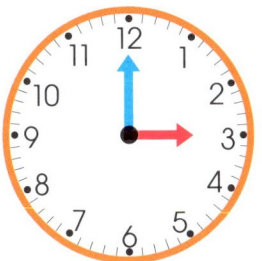

The hour hand points to **3**.
The time is **3 o'clock**, or **3:00**.

Circle the correct time under each clock.

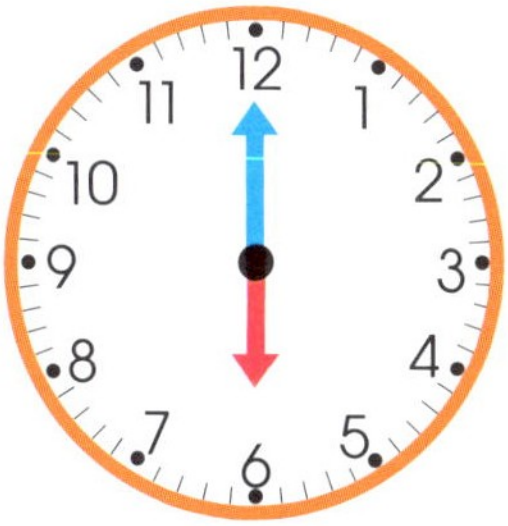

7:00
6:00
9:00

9:00
10:00
4:00

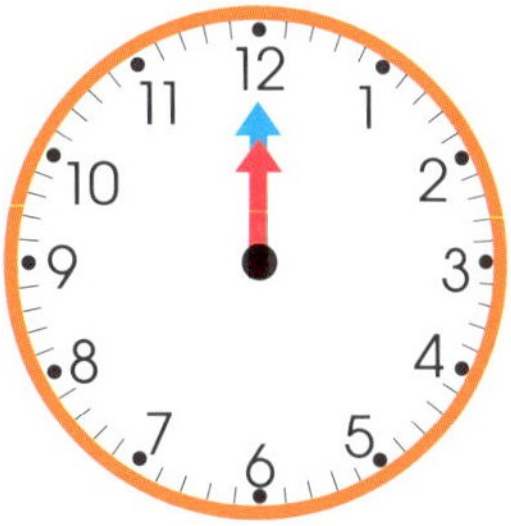

1:00
10:00
12:00

2:00
6:00
8:00

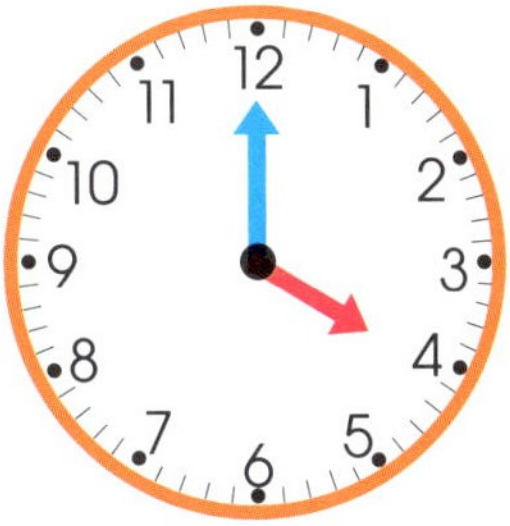

3:00
12:00
4:00

9:00
7:00
1:00

Circle what happens **next**.

Circle what happens **next**.

Circle the picture whose name **begins** with the **same sound** as the first one.

rain

duck

jack-o'-lantern

Circle the picture whose name **begins** with the **same sound** as the first one.

elephant

fire

pear

Circle the picture whose name **begins** with the **same sound** as the first one.

cow

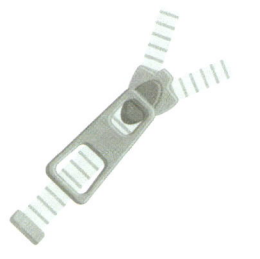
zipper

goat

Circle the picture whose name **begins** with the **same sound** as the first one.

hat

ostrich

apple

Circle the picture whose name **begins** with the **same sound** as the first one.

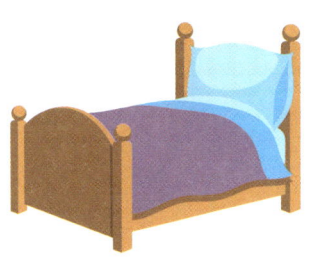
bed

turkey

saw

Circle the picture whose name **begins** with the **same sound** as the first one.

ladder

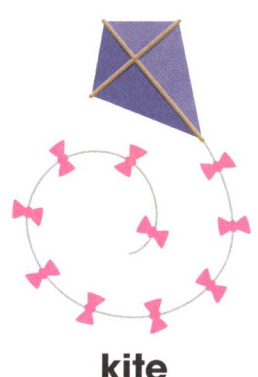
kite

mouse

Say the name of the picture.
Circle the letter that **begins** the picture's name.

Say the name of the picture.
Circle the letter that **begins** the picture's name.

Say the name of the picture.
Circle the letter that **begins** the picture's name.

Say the name of the picture.
Circle the letter that **begins** the picture's name.

Circle the word that is the **same** as the first one.

Circle the word that is the **same** as the first one.

Draw lines to match the **action words**.

run

hop

jump

run

fly

hop

fly

jump

Draw lines to match the **action words** to the correct sentences.

fly

I can jump.

hop

I can run.

run

I can hop.

I can fly.

jump